Returning to Dust

poems by

Carol Poster

Finishing Line Press
Georgetown, Kentucky

Returning to Dust

Copyright © 2017 by Carol Poster
ISBN 978-1-63534-338-0 First Edition
All rights reserved under International and Pan-American Copyright Conventions. No part of this book may be reproduced in any manner whatsoever without written permission from the publisher, except in the case of brief quotations embodied in critical articles and reviews.

ACKNOWLEDGMENTS

Poems in this collection have previously appeared in the following periodicals:

Aethlon: The Journal of Sport Literature
Asphodel
Avocet
Blue Unicorn
In Between Hangovers
Pea River Journal
Tapjoe
The Chaffin Journal
The Dead Mule School of Southern Literature
The Formalist
The Maine Review

Publisher: Leah Maines

Editor: Christen Kincaid

Cover Art: Carol Poster

Author Photo: Carol Poster

Cover Design: Elizabeth Maines McCleavy

Printed in the USA on acid-free paper.
Order online: www.finishinglinepress.com
also available on amazon.com

Author inquiries and mail orders:
Finishing Line Press
P. O. Box 1626
Georgetown, Kentucky 40324
U. S. A.

Table of Contents

I: Urban Artifacts
Complicity 1
Flirtation 2
The Incorruptible Dead 3
Aubade 4
Downsview Station, Toronto 5
The Play of Light on Form 6
Lucubrare 7
Images of Fire 8
Archaeological Survey 9
Returning to Dust 10

II: Oscillations
The Empty Plains 12
Early Migrations 13
On Pleasant Pastures Seen 14
Shapes of Dust 15
Images of the Moon 16
Conical Sections 17
Epicycles 18
Night Driving 19
National Traditions 20
Desert Wind 21

III: Deserted Landscapes
Electric Lake 24
Powell's First Rapid 25
San Rafael River below the Swinging Bridge 26
Sisyphus 27
Alien Species 28
Barren Lands 29
Baptism 30
Adaptation 31
Stillwater Canyon 32
Essence 33

I: Urban Artifacts

Complicity

Caught in the gusting wind,
a swallowtail flutters ahead.
The lights are red
for eight lanes in each direction,
leaving a vast emptiness
at the heart of the intersection,
except for a few left-turning SUVs,
and the butterfly,
buffeted by monsoon winds
from feeding on golden bells
in the median
to this oddly desolate space,
wings beating ineffectually.
Soon, the light will change
and I will drive forward
with the rest, complicit
in an ephemeral death.

Flirtation

Venus almost touched the moon tonight.
I can see her from my window seat
Near the false dawn.
She dances through the sky
attached to the sun,
retreating away and spinning back,
a celestial attraction,
forty-eight degrees
of apparent separation
at her most recalcitrant,
she circles the sun
and shines.

When I clear customs,
I'll turn on my phone
so we can meet
before centrifugal forces
return me home.

The Incorruptible Dead

Aristotle claimed the best witnesses
were the incorruptible dead,
their words true for all time,
unbribable, and not likely
to be cowed by threats.

They're the best lovers, too,
I suspect.
Unable to disappoint or betray,
not just the outlines but the details
of their lives
fixed for eternity.

From the beginning, you know
that Plato's not the marrying kind,
or that Aristotle, himself unfaithful,
was good to his wife.

Bodies corrupted, but spirits incorruptible,
steadfast for all time,
the dead offer
neither wedding vows nor children,
not domestic bliss,
nor even moments
of sensual pleasure

But they will return your love
with wisdom.
Mirrors sometimes shine
brighter than lights.

Aubade

Indigo morning brightens
My window.
A transmission line
Bifurcates the rectangle of light.
The lake is quiet.
The geese behind my cabin sleep,
And no wind rustles the trees.

You wake to traffic in the city somewhere,
Your right hand pulling back brown hair
From your forehead, fingers extended
And head tilted left.

You lean forward
Before you start to speak.
From your familiar gestures,
Words, bubbles of air, escape
Up as you look down,
Through blue water remote as the sky
Which fades from deep indigo to morning light.

Downsview Station, Toronto

The spindly trees, wrapped in winter burlap
like flocks of dead geese
impaled on wooden sticks,
were planted around the harshly brutalist station
not for beauty, but as a carbon footprint
reduction strategy.

Grey skies spit occasional snowflakes
at this scrap of industrial wasteland,
invisible on the glass and metal building.

Passengers in wet wool coats and toques
or dark hooded parkas
flow from subway to cars and buses
in orderly monochrome streams,
silent, heads down,
part of the desolation.

Perhaps some spring, unwrapped,
the trees will flourish,
exuberantly green and wildly growing,
sucking up fumes and pollution
in an anarchic rebellion,
musicians will busk in the parking lots,
and the wild geese return,
grey-brown but honking wildly,
to bear goslings on the highway median.

The Play of Light on Form

I see a pigeon lying dead beside the curb.
I imagine it as an eight by ten,
Notice I'd need to turn the image
A few degrees to make it work.

I'd stretch the unmarred wing across
The bottom of the picture,
The symmetry of its fluted form
Contrasting with the mangled head and torso.
I'd include just an inch or two of curb,
Artificially straight lines against the fluid curves.

The colours should be sombre, grey on grey,
Peaceful, just road and curb and feathers,
A study in black and white,
Fast film with coarse grain,
The dried blood, a zone 6 black,
And lines so pure
They would not need to be explained.

Lucubrare

Lucubrate, you said, is what we do,
Working on your computer late one night,
Like the Romans, who had a single word
For it, "*lucubrare,*" to work by candlelight.

I'm writing late, the evening of
St. Lucy's anniversary,
The longest night of the year,
When your words return to me.

I freeze, mid-sentence, remember how
In late winter nights, you were a beacon,
Of sorts, but are no more. As I remember,
The year turns; the dark is receding now.

Images of Fire

I search for meaning in your firelit face—
eyes, nose, mouth, the permutations of flesh,
communicate nothing.

Brown eyes, glasses, hair softened with strands
of grey, and your beard, smooth as a Siamese cat,
glow in the campfire warmth
against red rock and river sand.
I watch your silence,
which I try to understand.

These are not real.
I sit on a plastic chair in an urban coffee shop,
imagine you, the river, the fire, the campsite.
I've never camped on that river, nor with you,
and the scene I construct explains you no better
than the ambiguous flickering firelit face
I imagine.

Archaeological Survey
    San Juan County, Utah

The shapes appear to hold a meaning you
Almost see in certain angles of the light.
You could observe a human symmetry
In patterned shadows, or perhaps the bright
Sandstone could speak to you, give voice to those
Who farmed the same harsh land of scrub and brush
That you explore. The walls are broken. Cows
Kick down the standing masonry. They crush
Pots, corn cobs, all faint traces of the past
Inhabitants, compounding time's slow work
With quicker measures of their own—at least
Disturbing the stratigraphy. You walk
Past rocks and earthen mounds that nearly seem
Arranged, in certain light, that almost mean.

Returning to Dust

The desert reclaims the Frisco ghost town
Below the ridge where I am camping.
Creosote and hard-packed sand thread paths through piles
Of rust-colored rock, corroded metal, and desiccated timber,
Remains of the silver mine, houses, twenty-one saloons,
And a dance hall so respectable a young woman, attending alone,
Would not risk hearing a rude word.

Alone in the wilderness, I don't fear rude words
All of which I used when staking my tent,
And no major predators lurk in the high desert
Where small rodents barely sustain
The few raptors and coyotes.

"Two shots for two bits—"
Whiskey was cheaper than water
And a nickel bet was a killing matter,
Smith and Wesson reliably beating five aces,
Every time.

I watch from where the miners did
When the main shaft collapsed.
Settlers twenty miles away in Milford
Heard china tinkle as cabinets shook from the crash,
But no one was injured, directly.

Now the vultures circle in late afternoon thermals,
As if the crumpled houses and rusted mining gear
Were the carcass of some great creature
Laid out for their feasting.

II: Oscillations

The Empty Plains

An event horizon
is the edge
of a black hole.

It doesn't actually exist,
according to physicists,
except conceptually,
as a limit behind which
nothing happens,
or if anything does,
it doesn't matter,
for no information
escapes it.

In the US,
I used to think
it was near Nebraska,
but sandhill cranes
fly thousands of miles
to return to the Platte River
every summer.
So it's not there.

Perhaps it's in Iowa, or Kansas,
or even South Dakota.

I'm sure I've driven through it sometime
but I don't remember it.

Early Migrations

A smoky funnel undulates ahead,
Geese swirling in pointilliste patterns.
As I approach, dots resolve to angles
wings furling and unfurling in formation,
until, as I pass, they dissolve back
into a dark smoky swirl on the horizon
They coil and writhe like a stationary tornado.

Another cloud appears ahead,
not geese but smoke, wreathing a smokestack,
billowing in a puffy spiral,
that stretches towards lush southern marshes.

February is too early for migrations,
too bleak, too cold.
Asphalt unfurls through wheat stubble
I navigate alone,
as smoke coils, deceptively mobile,
through dormant fields
cleaved by a desolate road.

On Pleasant Pastures Seen

Stately turning windmills clump on barren fields
like drunken starlings perched in untidy gaggles.
Cylindrical metal towers and asymmetric blades
glow matte white in the fading sun.

They loom, oddly curved blades undulating,
vast cetaceans arcing through cerulean wind currents,
their measured pace eerily calm, oddly silent.

The world's sound masked by tire noise and metal casing,
rushing air blocked by windshield glass, I drive,
senses insulated from sound, smell, and weather.

Perhaps the blades howl as they turn,
albeit barely disturbing the cattle placidly grazing below,
oblivious to all but the frozen stubble
crackling under their hooves,
their warm scent wafted by the windmills
through brittle Kansas winter air.

Each single windmill is smoothly sinuous,
only an unsynchronized red link blinking
to disturb its symmetry.
Together though, they spin erratically,
a cacophony of random speeds and orientations,
the blinking lights and jagged movement
of a huge industrial city I cannot hear.

Perhaps the windmills clank or growl or wail.
I could stop to listen,
but as the sun sinks and the road darkens,
I dare not seek such knowledge.

Shapes of Dust

Through breaks in the billowing dirt road dust,
a shape ahead appears a fallen girl,
knees bent, arm outstretched, head turned aside,
hit by a truck or tossed from a pickup bed.

The pickup I'm following blocks the view,
and then I see the shape again,
a rotting deer with spotted skin,

As I draw level with the corpse,
deer flies, momentarily unsettled by the traffic,
spiral away in a billowing cloud of dust,
undulating like dark seaweed in a turbulent fjord.

In my rear view mirror, the deer recedes
into the amorphous mass
it will eventually become
as sun and rain and flies
consume its fleeting flesh.
We are dust. To dust we shall return.

Images of the Moon

I've set up my tripod under the bridge.
It's almost sunset. Downstream, a man fishes.
"I haven't had a bite all day," he says.
I meter the guard rail and start to shoot.
"I hope my fire doesn't ruin your pictures."
"Not at all." He piles on more wood.
"We've got a good hunter's moon tonight."
I kneel in the mud for a low angle shot.
"Big ring around it. Weather should be changing soon."
It needs a graduated neutral density filter times two.
"I can smell the snow in the air. It's overdue."

I could bring my sleeping bag down to the sand,
Watching the flickering fire and steady moon.
I'd sleep better here than I would at home.
The sky darkens to a saturated indigo,
And shadows to deep blue. I love to camp.
I drive back to town once the light has gone.

Conical Sections

A hawk spirals in wind currents east of the road,
Belly buff, wings and head brown, tilting deliberately
Inwards, not wavering like a vulture, but smoothly
Searching for movement in empty rangeland.
The cattle have moved to summer pastures.
Rodents and their predators, coyote, vulture,
Kit fox, and circling hawk are all that remain,
Left to hover over feathered sage, rice grass,
Straw bunch grasses stuck between round river stones,
And myself, fleeing to the wilderness, from the wilderness,
Oscillating between empty and figured landscapes,
A narrowing spiral from which there is no escape.

Epicycles

I run on frosted grass. My feet slide, leave
Black horseshoes where my toes have pushed the mud
Back. Fog blots the trees. Dead leaves cover
Part of the track. They're brown and flat, slippery too.
I avoid hard pavement, slick leaves, and ice,
Circle outside on the mowed grass instead,
Watch my step. I see mud patches,
Smeared by my feet on a previous lap,
Remember you, and think this time around
Would be no different than the last, know
The rain will wash the mud back into grass—
How little I affect the things I pass.

Night Driving

For the first few hours
I exercise exquisite care,
wrenching my car close
to dangerous drop-offs
to avoid deer mice, kangaroo
rats and several species
of ground squirrel.
Then I hit one, a small
rodent, not endangered
or even rare.
Next, a jackrabbit startles,
leaps directly under
my right front wheel
with a loud thump,
and I'm too tired to care.
Soon, I leave a trail
of blood behind me—
raccoons, gophers, lizards, voles.
Mesmerized by the inevitability
of these moonlit encounters,
I refuse to swerve
for anything smaller
than a mule deer.

National Traditions

After clearing Canadian customs,
I see a two-lane road,
with cows grazing the open range,
vegetation and landscape
just like Montana.
The car-body riprap,
roadside litter, and language
are the same,
the accents and metric system
only slightly strange,
the houses, gas stations, and silos
of similar design,
but even in Alberta
there are no bullet holes
in the road signs.

Desert Wind

The desert wind outside my window shouts.
Tree branches, desiccated by the rainless winter,
toss and rustle with eerily sibilant sounds.
The wind itself moans as it angles up the wash,
tenor crescendo diminishing to hollow baritone,
with crickets performing a monotonous percussion
in the background.
The wind shifts, striking my house head on.
The screen rattles against the sliding glass door.
I am fragile and alone.

III: Deserted Landscapes

Electric Lake

"We call it Electric Lake because when they put it in,
that's when we got the electric," says the ex-miner
who's towing my defunct Toyota out of the Swell.

"Didn't have the electric back in the mining days.
I drove up there every day from Price,
except Sundays, in the old Blazer.
They salted the hell out of the road.
Back's damn near rusted out, but she still runs.
I come out here a lot these days, across the wash.
Leave the new Buick for the wife at home.
Kids moved to Salt Lake a few years ago.
Guess there wasn't much for them to stay for—
even with the electric."

John Wesley Powell's First Rapid

Powell explores the river shore,
an ex-army captain, walking one-armed
through tamarisk, quicksand, and river willow,
scouting the rock-studded rapids,
where spilled boulders from a side canyon
constrict the river with flood debris,
all the cast-offs of the high desert,
dead pinyon and juniper branches,
tumbleweeds, clay sediments,
the occasional dead animal,
jackrabbit, mule deer, coyote, and kit fox,
snakes, lizards, the smaller rodents,
prey and predator mingled together,
usually just scraps of desiccated fur or bone
but sometimes a whole carcass,
with its hordes of scavengers,
vultures and ants, crows and black flies,
or boat crews seeking to supplement
monotonous rations.

Parched by hot sun in the rainless summer
corpses dry out rather than rot
leaving bleached bones by crumbling rock
before the first rapid, Disaster Falls,
where dories swing in the current,
planks shatter,
and men fall
into seething water.

San Rafael River below the Swinging Bridge

The river ripples through a rock garden,
Shallow and slow, beneath some small rapids.
Even in this remote meander,
The water foams
Like mold on bread kept out too long,
Alkali salts spot the muddy bottom.
Cottonwoods and tamarisks line the banks.
Above, massive Wingate cliffs crumble to bloody silt,
Blending with the softly eroded Chinle layer,
Soft purple and green clay like a faint bruise
Fading into pale brown sand,
Surrounded by the faint chemical smell
Of cow manure decomposing
Back into the land.

Sisyphus

The ground slides under my foot.
My leg wobbles, shifts, until my weight
compresses the fluid sand to a solid.
Another step.
The dune's surface moves downhill
under me as I walk up.
It's like running in place on a waterbed,
only hotter. My forehead drips.
The dune looms over me, each sand grain
brilliant with reflected sun.
Sweat stings my eyes,
salt water I return to this remnant
of an ancient ocean.

Alien Species

The magpie flirts with the tamarisk branches,
flashing white stripes as he flips back his wings.
He perches. His black tail twitches nervously,
and his head cocks, watching me pitch my tent.
Our ancestors migrated here,
His earlier, mine more recently, both uninvited.

I rehydrate dinner. Soon, it will be dark.
The bird is alert, perhaps seeking a place
To roost for the night, or perhaps
Disturbed by my presence

The sun angles through the leaves
in isolated beams, picking out my stove,
a tent stake, and my meal.
The magpie searches for something to steal.

I clean dishes and teeth, crawl into my tent,
adjusting my foam pad and sleeping bag
to avoid tree roots inevitably unavoidable.
Feathery tamarisk brushes against the rainfly
As the stars gradually appear.

Intruders all, magpie, tamarisk, and human
settle into the dusk, as the temperature drops
and the canyon winds pick up.
I shiver. The tamarisk rustles. The magpie has vanished.

We do not belong here.

Barren Lands

I travel rivers to the Arctic, seek
The barren lands, a treeless waste beneath
The northern lights, with lichen-covered rock,
Thick mosses, and dark shrubs with waxy leaves.
I imagine these. I scramble up talus to reach
Alpine tundra, hike up past the trees,
Past a recent slide—rock piled on broken rock—
Shattered and cracked from its fall. I slip, then rise,
Hands bleeding slightly, crest a serrated ridge,
Spit on the stinging scrapes, then wipe them clean
On filthy climbing pants, and rearrange
My pack, finally top the *nevé* covered peak.
These too are barren lands, almost as far
Above the trees as the other ones are north.

Baptism

> *"You cannot step twice into the same river, for different and different waters flow."* Heraclitus.

Constantly new waters flow
Over a small waterfall.
Your chapped hands cup your chin
As you observe their motion.

Tongues of water collapse towards a whirlpool,
Exploding in incoherent foam,
As memories surge over consciousness,
Too swift to catch in language.

If one has harmed you by neglect
Or by deliberate action,
Let the tumbling water on rock
Wash away emotion.

Adaptation

I drift.
My canoe finds a channel,
meandering under the high desert sun,
sky deep altitude blue,
reflected on water brown with sandstone mud.

A curled bow wake peels back
from the straight stem,
pale apricot beneath ash rails,
sixteen feet long, frail, narrow, and sleek,
with extreme tumblehome,
designed to race,
the canoe drifts unsteadily,
as if nervous
about this leisurely progress.

Bow and stern are filled
by gear stowed in two
bright yellow river bags,
neatly tied in.
After this many river miles,
things finally fit.

Stillwater Canyon

sandstone
cliffs reflect
in water
under full
moon

a deep chasm
in the river
inverted
but still
true

Essence

> *Tel qu'en Lui-même enfin l'éternité le change ...*

I love best what my love cannot make stay.
Diagonal light textures bare rock and sand
As the sudden twilight ends the desert day.

The morning frost creates a crystalline plain,
Glitters with fragile beauty until it melts.
I love best what my love cannot make stay.

A swollen moon rises above rocks and sage,
Huge, casting faint blue shadows on the land,
As the sudden twilight ends the desert day.

Buff sandstone explodes into golden flames
As fleeting dawn mist rises from the sand.
I love best what my love cannot make stay.

Contorted rocks glow bronze when the final blaze
Of orange light turns pinyons to burning brands
As the sudden twilight ends the desert day.

Your face is gaunt, inessentials burnt away.
Your work consumes your life. Soon it will end
As the sudden twilight ends the desert day.
I love best what my love cannot make stay.

Carol Poster is the author of three chapbooks of poetry and three books of commercial nonfiction about outdoor recreation. Her poetry translations include *Selected Poems of Jacques Prévert* (White Pine Press), Platus' *Stichus* (Johns Hopkins University Press Complete Roman Drama series), and Aristophanes' *Clouds* (University of Pennsylvania Press Complete Greek Drama). She has also published nonfiction widely in magazines and web venues on topics as diverse as skiing, backpacking, computer technology, video games, real estate, and green lifestyles.

Poster has been writing for publication since she was a teenager. After graduating from Hollins University, she worked for a decade in the computer industry, first for Fortune 500 companies and then as a founder of her own consulting and software development firm, while continuing to write. Next, she returned to school for an MFA in Creative Writing (Eastern Washington University) and PhD in Rhetoric (University of Missouri), publishing substantial amounts of scholarship on ancient rhetoric and rhetoric of religion and teaching at University of Northern Iowa, Montana State University, Florida State University, and York University (Canada) before returning to freelance writing and photography.

Her poems, translations, and works of short fiction have appeared in periodicals including *Avocet, The Ball State University Forum, Bitterroot, Blue Unicorn, The Formalist, Hampden-Sydney Poetry Review, Hyperion, Kansas Quarterly, The Literary Review, Longhouse, The MacGuffin, The Maine Review, Outerbridge, Ploughshares,* and *Poetry East.*

www.ingramcontent.com/pod-product-compliance
Lightning Source LLC
LaVergne TN
LVHW050045090426
835510LV00043B/3205